Reading
Practice

GW01550992

Exercises devised by Brenda Apsley
an experienced author and editor who specialises
in writing early learning books for children
Illustrated by John Haslam

Learning Rewards is a home-learning programme designed to help your child succeed at school with the National Curriculum. It has been extensively researched with parents and teachers.

This book, *Reading Practice*, and its companion title, *Reading Skills*, cover important aspects of the National Curriculum at Key Stage I.

Children should start with the *Skills* books (with younger children this is important) and progress to the *Practice* books.

The *Skills* book teaches basic skills and new concepts through structured and enjoyable activities. The *Practice* book reinforces and builds on these skills by the essential repetition of exercises.

You will need to work through each page with your child and talk about what is required. The star symbol at the top of the page details the particular skills covered by the exercise as they relate to the National Curriculum. The content is progressive, so explain the importance of starting from the front of the book.

The fold-out progress chart is a useful record of your child's performance. Always reward your child's work with encouragement and a gold star sticker.

When you come to the end of the book you will find a fun, wipe-clean learning game.

series editor: Nina Filipek
series designer: Paul Dronsfield
designer: Hilary Edwards-Malam
Copyright © 1996 World International Limited.
All rights reserved.
Published in Great Britain by
World International Limited, Deanway Technology Centre,
Wilmslow Road, Handforth, Cheshire SK9 3FB.
Printed in Italy.
ISBN 0 7498 2710 6

WORLD

People

To read familiar words, building a basic reading vocabulary.

Read the words on the balloons.
Choose four words that describe you.
Write the words on the empty balloons.

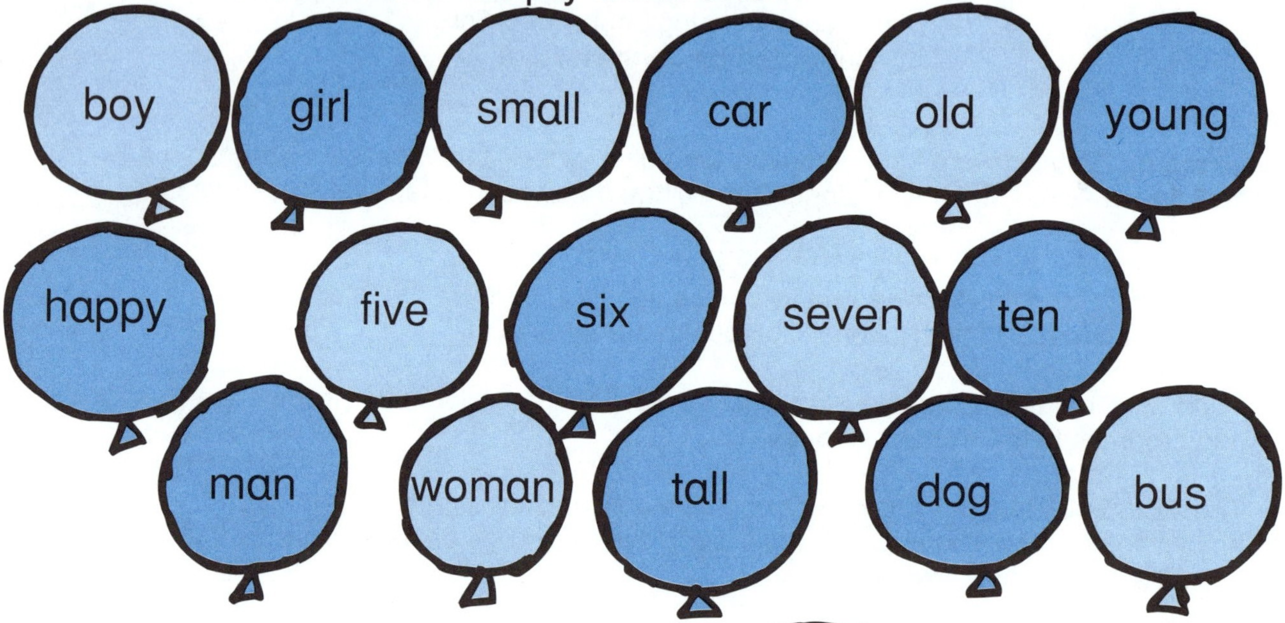

boy girl small car old young

happy five six seven ten

man woman tall dog bus

Words about me.

Tick the family words.

brother brown sink dad bad sister mum
☑

Reading

☆ To read familiar words accurately and make appropriate choices.

Look at the picture of the bedroom.
Read the words. Tick the things you can see in the bedroom.

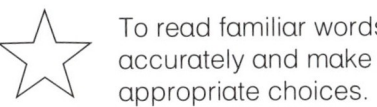

lamp	lion	clock	bed	top	tiger	rug
☐	☐	☐	☐	☐	☐	☐

boot	bag	door	chair	rag	toy	book
☐	☐	☐	☐	☐	☐	☐

3

Numbers

Read the words. Cross out the word in each set that is NOT a number word.

| two | for | tree | on | five |
| too | four | three | one | file |

| stick | seen | egg | nine | ten |
| six | seven | eight | none | tent |

Read the number rhyme. Write the missing number words on the lines. Choose from the list.

One little, two little,

_____ little teddy bears,

Four little, _____ little,

_____ little teddy bears.

_____ little, eight little,

_____ little teddy bears,

_____ little teddy bear friends.

seven   ten

nine   five

three   six

To read number words up to twenty.

Write the numeral for each number word. The first one is done to show you how.

13		17
20		16
11		19
18		14
12		15

eleven   11

twelve _____

thirteen _____

fourteen _____

fifteen _____

sixteen _____

seventeen _____

eighteen _____

nineteen _____

twenty _____

Tick the words that match the picture.

twelve birds ☐

thirteen birds ☐

four trees ☐

fourteen trees ☐

eleven floors ☐

eleven flowers ☐

two goats ☐

two gates ☐

5

Weather

To read weather words, and answer questions that test comprehension.

Read the words. Tick the weather words.

storm ✓   stone ☐   store ☐

frog ☐   fog ☐   log ☐

wild ☐   win ☐   wind ☐

slow ☐   snow ☐   show ☐

Draw lines to match the sentence halves.

Sun is   cold.

Rain is   hot.

Ice is   wet.

Read the weather words. Draw pictures.

A windy day.

A rainy day.

Reading

 To read weather words and collect information from a chart.

Here is a weather chart.
Read the weather words, then answer the questions.

Monday	hot	sunny	
Tuesday	rainy		
Wednesday	cloudy		
Thursday	warm		
Friday	windy	rainy	

Did it rain on Monday? _____

Which day was hot and sunny? _____

Which day was cloudy?_____

What was Friday's weather like?_____

Which days were rainy? _____

7

Colours

To read colour words and follow instructions accurately.

Hello! I am a moon monster.
I lost my colours in the rain.
Will you put them back for me?

Colour my hair green.
Colour my T-shirt red and blue.
Colour my hat pink.
Colour my trousers orange with black spots.

Colour my boots brown.
Colour my skin yellow.

Tick the colour words.

grin ☐	blow ☐	black ☐	purse ☐
grey ☐	brown ☐	back ☐	purple ☐

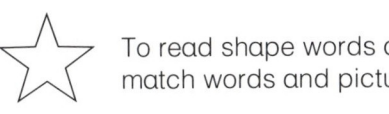 To read shape words and to match words and pictures.

Draw lines to match the words to the shapes in the picture.

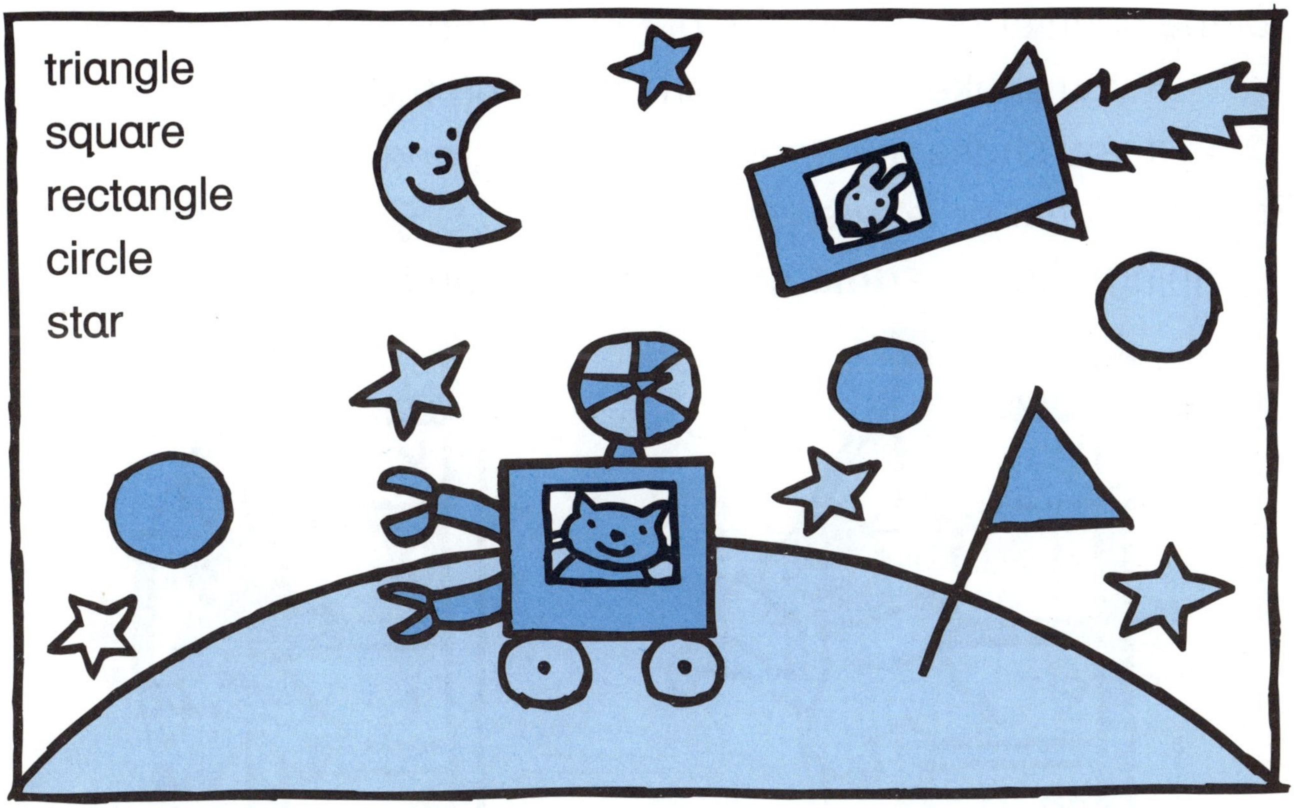

triangle
square
rectangle
circle
star

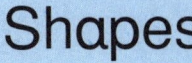

Tick the words that match the pictures.

two cubes ☐	four squares ☐	three cubes ☐
two circles ☐	four hearts ☐	three cones ☐

Word game

To recognise and match letter sounds and to read and follow instructions.

Play this word game. You will need a die and a counter.
Put the counter at the bottom of the first ladder. Shake the die.

If you shake a 1, move one place up the ladder.

If you shake a 2, move two places, and so on.

Read the letter or letters where you land. Say **two** words beginning with the **same sound** before you throw again.

10

To recognise and match letter sounds and to read and follow instructions.

Word game

When you get to the top of the first ladder, slide down the rope and climb to the top of the second ladder. Play until you have climbed the last ladder to z.

Ladder 1 (bottom to top):
l
m
n
o
p
pl
q
r
s
sh

Ladder 2 (bottom to top):
sl
st
t
tr
u
v
w
x
y
z
FINISH

Clothes

☆ To read clothes words and follow instructions accurately.

Choose the right word to finish the sentences. Write on the lines.

I wear a sock on each _____.	feet	flat	foot
I wear mittens on my _____.	head	hands	heels
I wear _____ on my feet.	books	balls	boots

Tick two words in each set.

I wear these on my feet.	shoes ☐	vest ☐	socks ☐
I wear these on my head.	cap ☐	coat ☐	hat ☐
I wear no clothes here.	shop ☐	bath ☐	shower ☐

Colour pairs of socks with the same word on them.
Choose a different colour for each pair.

To read clothes words and make appropriate choices.

Clothes

Polly has lots of clothes to put away.

Read the words on each drawer to see what goes inside.

Draw lines to put the clothes in the right drawers.

1	jeans
2	vest
3	belt
4	jumper
5	dress
6	T-shirt
7	shoes
8	hat

What goes in drawer 7? _____

Do jeans or jumpers go in drawer 1? _____

Do T-shirts go in drawer 3? _____

A story

To read a traditional story in rebus form and answer questions that test comprehension.

Read this story out loud. It is written in words and pictures.

The Lion and the Mouse

Once upon a time, 🦁 was asleep. 🐭 ran along his nose and woke him. Lion put his big 🐾 on Mouse. He opened his 😮 to eat him.

"Let me go," said 🐭 .

"Why?" asked Lion.

"If you help me I will help you," said Mouse.

🦁 smiled and let him go.

Later, bad 👦👦 tied Lion to a 🌳 with 🪢 .

Mouse cut the ropes with his 🐭 .

Lion was free. "Thank you, little friend," he said.

"I said I would help you," said 🐭 . "Didn't I?"

Answer these questions about the story. Tick the right words.

Who was asleep?   Lion ☐   Mouse ☐

Who tied Lion up?   bad mice ☐   bad people ☐

What did Mouse cut with his teeth?   rolls ☐   ropes ☐

Reading

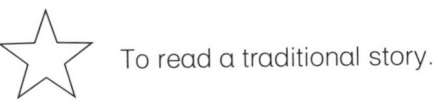 To read a traditional story.

The pictures tell the story. **The Ugly Duckling**

Look at the pictures and try to read the sentences.

① Mother Duck had two little ducklings and one big duckling.

② The little ducklings made fun of the big duckling.

③ The ugly duckling ran away.

④ The ugly duckling was all alone.

⑤ The ugly duckling looked in the water.

⑥ The ugly duckling was now a lovely white swan!

Holidays

To read holiday words and make choices that test reading accuracy and comprehension.

Kim is on holiday at the seaside. She has sent a postcard to her friend. Read the postcard. Kim wrote it in words and pictures.

Dear Katy

Today I went in the  .

It was cold! I made a .

I put shells on it and a on top.

I sat under a big to

eat my . A

tried to take it!

Love from

Kim

Katy Mills
3 Bank Road
Hill Town
HI3 2BA

What is Kim's friend called? _____

What did Kim put on top of her sand castle? _____

Who tried to steal Kim's ice cream? _____

Read these holiday words.

sand castle   flag   ice cream   seagull

 To interpret information from a chart.

Holidays

Class Two made a travel chart. They found out if people went on holiday by car, train, plane, bus or boat.

How many people went by train? _____

Did anyone go on a boat? _____

How did most people travel? _____

Follow the lines to find out where the children went on holiday.

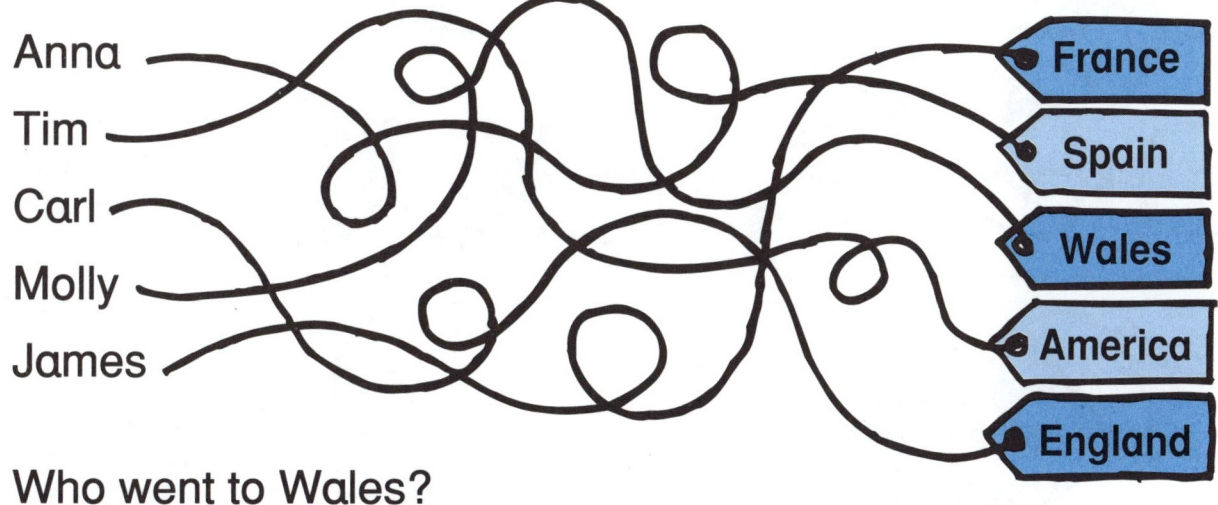

Who went to Wales? _____

Where did Tim go? _____

Did Anna go to France or Spain? _____

Food

To read food words, and match instructions and pictures.

Class Two are having a baking day. They are going to make cookies. Read how to make cookies. Match the instructions to the pictures. Write a number for each picture.

Cookies

You need:

100g butter
100g sugar
2 eggs
300g flour

1. Put everything in a bowl.
2. Mix with a spoon.
3. Roll out the mixture.
4. Cut into shapes.

To read food words, and match words and pictures.

Where do you go to buy food? Tick the right word.

bank ☐   school ☐   supermarket ☐   post office ☐

At the supermarket you can see lots of food words.
Draw lines to match the pictures to the words.

eggs

yogurt

milk

fish

bread

fruit

vegetables

tins of soup

Days and months

 To read the names of days of the week and months of the year.

Read the days of the week. Write the missing days in the diary. Choose from the list.

Thursday
Monday
Saturday
Tuesday

Read the months of the year.

January	February	March	April
May	June	July	August
September	October	November	December

What is the first month of the year? _____

Which month comes before November? _____

What month comes after May? _____

What month is your birthday? _____

What month is it now? _____

20

To read the names of the
seasons of the year.

Find the names of the seasons in the word square. Look left to
right, right to left, and up and down. Draw rings around the words.

S	P	R	I	N	G
U	A	E	F	M	B
M	O	T	G	U	C
M	P	N	D	T	H
E	J	I	M	U	N
R	S	W	L	A	K

SPRING

SUMMER

AUTUMN

WINTER

Now find the days of the
week in this word square.

A	B	M	P	T	N	R	O	S	A
W	S	A	T	U	R	D	A	Y	B
E	C	E	D	E	L	O	P	A	B
D	J	F	K	S	N	T	U	D	R
N	S	U	N	D	A	Y	Q	S	T
E	G	D	M	A	R	S	V	R	L
S	H	C	B	Y	X	T	W	U	N
D	I	F	R	I	D	A	Y	H	X
A	J	K	A	L	Z	U	Y	T	O
Y	A	D	N	O	M	V	W	X	P

SUNDAY

MONDAY

TUESDAY

WEDNESDAY

THURSDAY

FRIDAY

SATURDAY

Farm

To read farm words and answer questions that test general knowledge.

Draw lines to match the farm words to the things in the picture.

farm house  tractor

stable   fence

farmer   field

pond   gate

Read the baby animal words.
Choose words from the list to finish the sentences.

calf   chick   lamb   foal

A baby hen is a _____.

A baby cow is a_____.

A baby horse is a _____.

A baby sheep is a _____.

To read animal words and answer questions that test general knowledge.

Read the animal names.

bat	moth	bird	fox
owl	horse	bee	hen

Write the animals that come out in the day under DAY.
Write the animals that come out at night under NIGHT.

DAY
bird

NIGHT

Draw lines to match the animals to their homes.

rabbit

bee

bird

hive

nest

burrow

Wild animals

To read wild animal words and solve puzzles that test reasoning and general knowledge.

Read the wild animal words.

lion
camel
octopus
dolphin
fish
snake
whale
tiger

Colour the animals with four legs yellow.
Colour the animals that live in water blue.
Choose a colour for the animal that is left.

Tick the word in each set that is an animal.

| mole ☐ | bean ☐ | fish ☐ | shark ☐ | lion ☐ |
| mop ☐ | bear ☐ | fist ☐ | shock ☐ | line ☐ |

Reading

To read wild animal words, and solve puzzles that test reasoning and general knowledge.

Read the animal names.

Write the animals that live in hot places under HOT.

Write the animals that live in cold places under COLD.

HOT   **COLD**

camel	polar bear
elephant	penguin
monkey	seal
reindeer	zebra

Finish the sentences about animals.

Draw lines to match the two parts that go together.

A snail has a   eight legs.

An octopus has   black and white.

A seal can   fly.

A bat can   swim.

A zebra is   shell.

Information books

Class Two use books in the school library to help them find out about things. They use a set of six information books.

They find out about space in book 5, under **s**.
They find out about water in book 6, under **w**.

Write the number of the book where you will find out about these things.

trees 5   bears ☐

football ☐   zoos ☐

snakes ☐   aircraft ☐

26

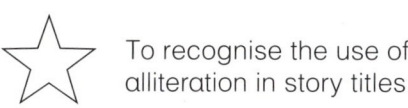 To recognise the use of alliteration in story titles.

Here are some story book titles. Part of each title is missing. Find words that start with the same letter. Write them on the lines. Remember that names start with capital letters.

Cookie the __Clown__   Rabbit

_____ in Pink Pyjamas   Bear

Rosie the _____   Dilly

Bill the _____   Panda

_____ the Dinosaur   Clown

Read the story book titles. Draw a picture for each one.

Sam the Snowman

Moop the Moon Monster

School sports day

To read a notice and answer questions that test reading accuracy and comprehension.

Here is a poster for the sports day at Old Lane School.
Write in the missing words. Choose from the list.

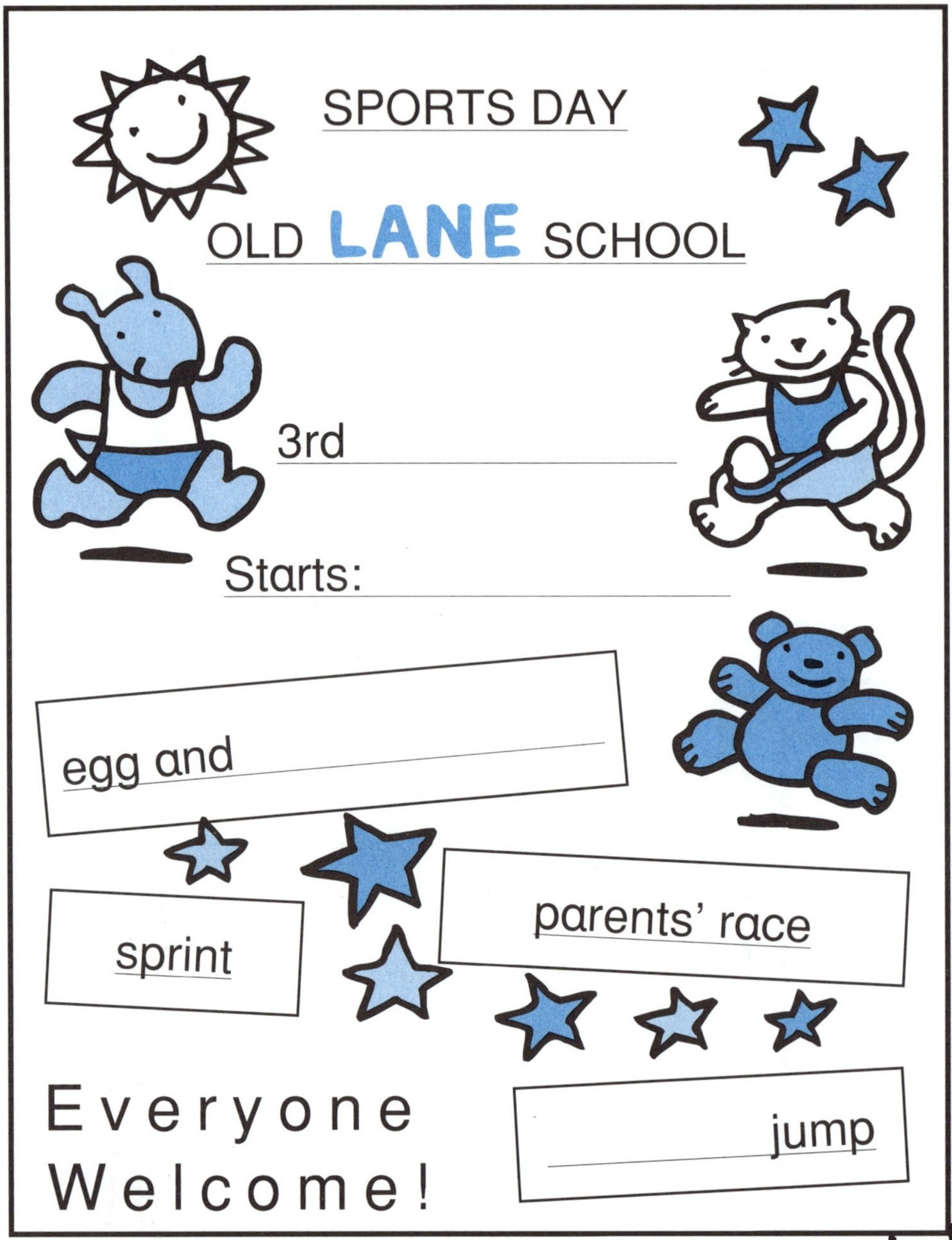
SPORTS DAY
OLD LANE SCHOOL
3rd
Starts:
egg and
sprint
parents' race
Everyone Welcome!
jump

LANE

long

July

12 o'clock

spoon race

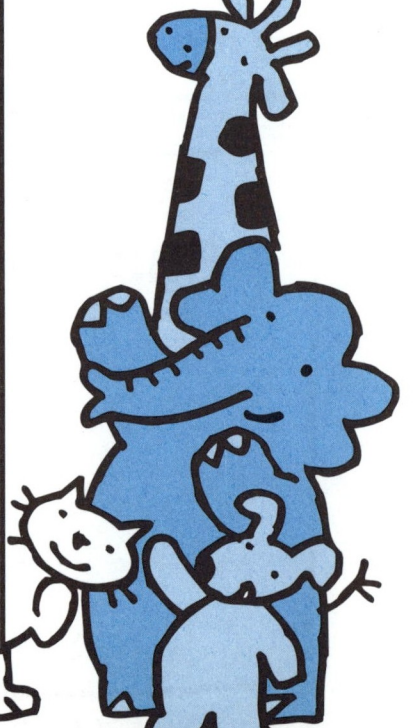

Reading

 To tell a story from pictures and answer questions that test comprehension.

The pictures tell a story about the egg and spoon race.

Look at the pictures and answer the questions.

How many were in the race? _____

How many boys were in the race? _____

What did the children have on spoons? _____

Who lost his egg first? _____

Who won the race? _____

Verbs

To read and match sentence halves to test reading accuracy and observation.

Molly and her friends went to the playground.

Look at the picture. Draw lines to make sentences.

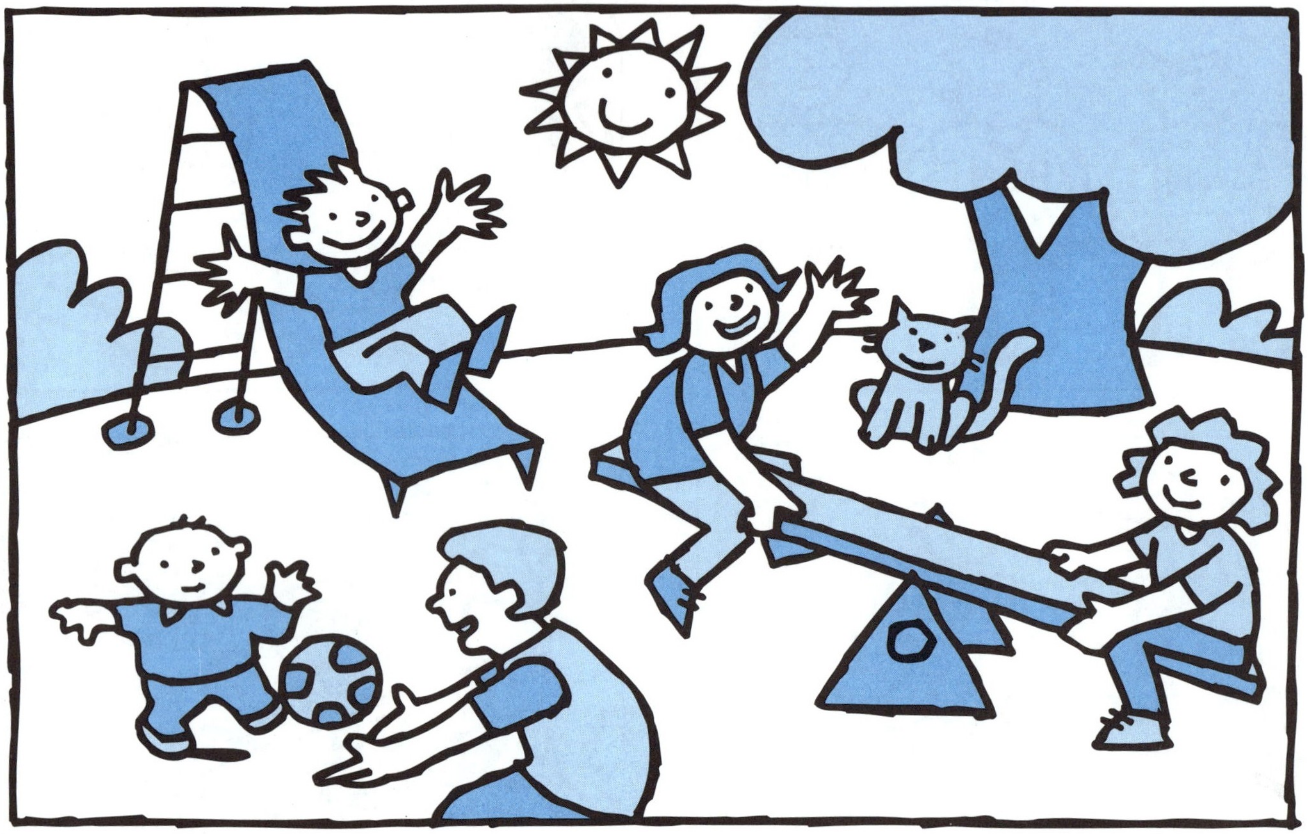

One boy slides	a ball.
Two girls are playing	under the tree.
A cat sits	down the slide.
A baby kicks	on the see-saw.

Reading

To read and match rhyming words and to read instructions accurately.

Here is a wall of bricks. Some of the words on the bricks rhyme. They sound the same, like **run**, **sun** and **bun**.

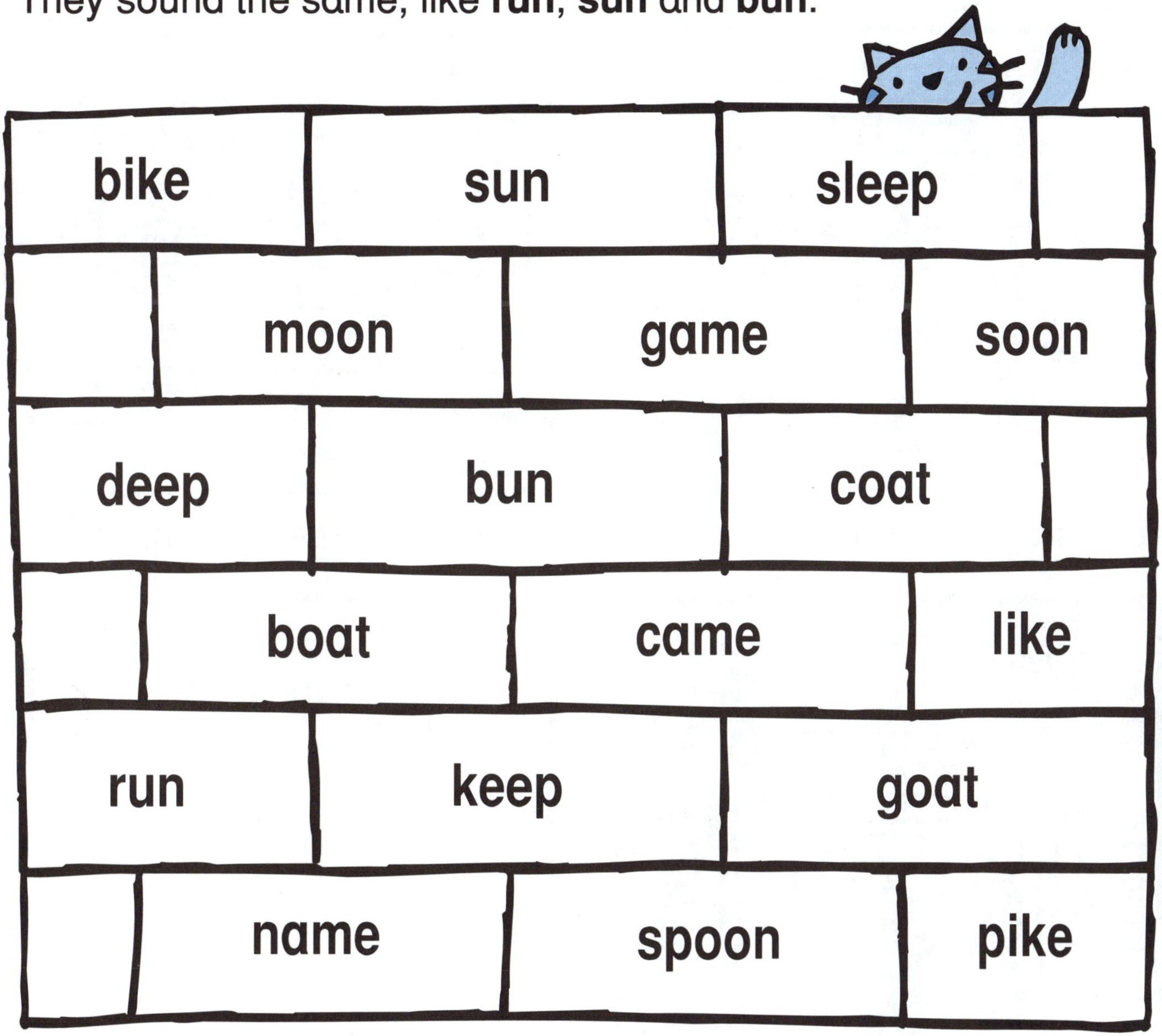

bike	sun	sleep

moon	game	soon

deep	bun	coat

boat	came	like

run	keep	goat

name	spoon	pike

Colour the word bricks that rhyme the same colour.

Signs

To read and understand familiar information signs.

Read the words under the pictures.
Tick the right word for each picture.

bus stop ☐ shop ☐ school ☐

cafe ☐ bank ☐ cinema ☐

library ☐ cinema ☐ station ☐

Draw a picture to match the sign.